CREATIVE
DRAMA
for
PRIMARY
SCHOOLS

CREATIVE DRAMA for PRIMARY SCHOOLS

A HANDBOOK OF ACTIVITIES

by Donald Lightwood

BLACKIE   Glasgow & London

Blackie & Son Limited
14–18 High Holborn, London WCIV 6BX
Bishopbriggs, Glasgow G64 2NZ

© Donald Lightwood 1970
First Published 1970
ISBN 0 216 88954 5

Printed in Great Britain by
R. & R. Clark Ltd., Edinburgh

CONTENTS

Introduction

It is now accepted that drama is a valuable aid in primary education and particular emphasis is laid on improvised dramatic activities, as opposed to the acting of scripted plays. A teacher may well agree with this, but be unsure of how to start improvised work. That is the reason for this book. It is to provide the primary teacher with practical ideas for improvised dramatic work.

The activities are divided into three sections: Movement; Mime; Improvised Plays. They will overlap in the drama lesson and it is desirable that they should. However this progression is a reasonable indication of how the work develops over a period of time, *and* in an individual lesson. This can best be seen if we consider the method on which the work is based.

The ability to control the body is fundamental if we are to achieve self confidence: one needs to be able to stand on one's own feet both literally and metaphorically. Nervous tension manifests itself physically. (And it should be remembered that speech is a physical act.) Rid the body of nervous tension, encourage control, and then you have the possibility of the imagination expressing itself in terms of movement and speech. In the Movement and Mime activities we are encouraging confidence and control, providing the children with an instrument capable of playing their improvised tune.

1

The progression in the lesson provides a solid framework on which to build. Movement activities utilize and harness the children's first burst of energy, and prepares them for the more detailed control necessary in Mime. The discipline of Mime, in turn, tones them up for work on Improvised Plays.

Drama can be introduced into the primary age range at any stage. The presentation will alter slightly according to age, but the activities remain the same. The main factor controlling the content and length of a lesson is the amount of experience the children have had, not their ages.

Look for what they respond to and enjoy. This will provide you with the key to your planning. From this you will gradually 'work outwards', embracing the other aspects of the work, and so build on a firm foundation. If your class enjoys singing, or playing percussion instruments, they may well incline towards rhythmical movement and dance; if keen on gym, athletic movement activities. If the children tend to be quiet and shy, the key to their enjoyment and interest may be pair mime games.

Whatever your approach, keep in mind that the goal is reached by way of confidence through physical control.

As an aid to the implementation of the ideas put forward in this book, three graded sets of workcards* have been produced to help organize group activities. Each card contains material designed to stimulate and occupy a group of about six children. In effect the workcards replace the pupils' book that one might expect as a companion to this volume. It is hoped that this departure will increase the scope of the children's own creative work, whilst retaining the feeling of spontaneity often found lacking in textbook work.

* Set 1 *Mime and Movement*. Set 2 *Stories for Acting*. Set 3 *Play Making*

Movement

Use the largest floor area available for all activities

Things to be   (whole class)

Change from one to the other rapidly, giving start and stop signals on the tambourine. Use children's suggestions when these are forthcoming.

1 Kings and Queens   Trees   Pirates
   Lumberjacks   Clowns   Lamp posts
   Old Men and Women   Horses   Chairs
   Skaters   Motor bikes   Fireworks
   Roadmenders   Spacemen   Ghosts

The teacher can add or subtract 'things' as she pleases, depending on the progress of the lesson. Children enjoy jumping from one 'thing' to another and the teacher can help this by having the class 'freeze' each 'thing' before moving on to the next, the command to freeze being a tap on the tambourine. This way the activity becomes a game, with the children doing their best not to be caught out.

Training the children to stop on command is important. It is impossible to conduct a large group in a free activity if there is no sense of group discipline. Obviously the teacher should not be harsh in instilling a regard for discipline: rather she should achieve the right response by making her commands enjoyable to carry out. 'Freezing' is an example of this. It works because it is positive, rather than negative ('Do' not 'Don't') and it makes use of the children's sense of fun. With care the teacher can solve all her problems of discipline in this way. Stated simply: if the rules are fun, the children will not want to break them.

2 BE Animals in the zoo
   Allow the class to act animals suggested by the children. Alternate boisterous animals with less active ones, e.g. monkeys; snakes; lions; seals; kangaroos; giraffes, etc.

3 BE The Tallest people in the world
   The Smallest

The Fattest	The Thinnest
The Loudest	The Quietest
The Fastest	The Slowest
The Strongest	The Weakest
The Happiest	The Stillest

4 BE Angry   Frightened   Brave   Evil   Happy   Sad
   Happy again

5 BE Hot   Cold   The Wind   The Sea   Snow   The Sun

6 BE Anything you like
   Act with a partner if you want to.

7 What would you like to be again? If a suggestion is promising, lead the activity towards a simple mime for the whole class, e.g.
   Lumberjacks felling trees, transporting the logs overland and by river to the saw-mill. (The children act being the lumberjacks, the trees, the logs, bulldozers, horses . . . they become everything they invent.)
   Fishermen in boats in a rough sea
   A circus
   A fairground

The Maze Game   (whole class)

1 Divide the class into two groups. Position one group in the centre of the hall, with at least an arm's length between each child. When positioned, the group stands like skittles. The

other group then has to weave its way backwards and forwards through the maze, without touching a skittle, or each other. If anyone touches, he is out.

2 Repeat, changing groups over. The group with the least number of touches is the winner.

Developments from the Maze Game

The Maze can be turned into a variety of different obstacles, e.g. enchanted wood; swamp; lamp posts; milk bottles, etc. So too the people, or animals, who have to overcome the obstacles, e.g. hunters; Indians; policemen; cats.

The next step could be a mime for the whole class, e.g. Indians hunting in the forest; carrying the catch back to their village; preparing and cooking it; holding a celebration feast.

The children will quickly understand the idea behind the maze situation and should be allowed to try out their own suggestions.

The Backwards and Forwards Game (whole class)

This game is a simple development from *Things to be*. Divide the class into two groups and line them up facing each other across the hall. Explain the tambourine signals: one tap = about-turn, two taps = stop still. The group move towards, and through each other, about-turning on reaching the opposite side of the hall. This basic pattern of movement is regularly interrupted by the tambourine, ordering unexpected about-turns. Periodically the teacher signals stop still: and then re-starts by giving a change of character.

It helps the fun if the characters are varied, e.g. man, animal; fast, slow; fat, thin; big, small.

If anyone touches he is out.

If the 'outs' number more than those left 'in', stop the in-children when they are suitably dispersed, and quickly order the out-children to run through the maze without touching. Order stop still, and re-start with the out-children as the maze.

Repeat, changing characters.

Balance Movement   (whole class)

Tambourine signals: make one movement on one sound. If it is a loud sound, make a big movement. If it is a quiet sound, make a small movement. After the movement, stay still and balanced until the next sound.

1 *Free movement* Start with the class scattered about the hall and standing absolutely still. (An atmosphere of suspense will help sharpen reactions.) Vary the volume of the tambourine signals and allow the children to move freely about the hall. Trying not to be caught out (i.e. off balance) will add fun.

2 *Growing* The children make themselves as small as they can. On each tap of the tambourine they make one growing movement until they are very tall.
Reverse the sequence, growing smaller.

3 *Growing in small groups* Each group chooses something that grows bigger and mimes it as a group, with or without help from the tambourine, e.g. flowers; trees; balloons; tyres.

4 *Fighting* (The aim is to encourage a stylized fighting in which the combatants do not touch each other. This activity is very close to free dance and requires an excellent sense of balance.) Divide the class into pairs. Work strictly to the tambourine, making only one fight movement on each tap, then hold balance. Various mimed weapons can be used, e.g. swords; daggers; battleaxes; quarter staffs; spears.

8

A fight can be ended with one or both of the fighters 'dying' on the teacher's counting up to four on the last four taps. Once again an atmosphere of suspense is very helpful.

Slow Motion   (whole class)

Slow motion movement can be used in many exercises. It is extremely useful as it imposes the need for more careful control, both in movement involving the whole body, and small detailed movement, as in hand mime. It will also be found to be beneficial as a calming influence on an excited class. For example, it takes only a tap on the tambourine to change a boisterous herd of animals into divers slowly (and silently) plodding along the sea bed.

1   Alternate marching at normal speed with marching in slow motion, using the tambourine signals: one tap = normal speed; two taps = slow motion; three taps = stop still.

2   As 1, adding an extra speed, skipping. Use the tambourine signal: one long tap and two short.

3   As 1 and 2, then gradually increase the frequency of normal speed with slow motion. These will get closer and closer together until they fuse into the skipping signal. Aim at achieving the same amount of control the children had in slow motion.

4   As 1, adding changes of characters for the children to act at the two speeds. Ask the class for people, animals or things, which move slowly and carefully. Some suggestions might be: Indians stalking; space men; cats; tortoises; seaweed; people in dreams.
Experiment, making quick things move slowly.

5   Sports in slow motion. As 1, changing sports. Good sports using the whole body rhythmically are: netball; tennis; football; throwing the javelin; fencing.

9

6   Use slow motion at any point in the lesson, e.g. for bridging two activities; moving the children into well-spaced positions or groups.

Machines   (whole class)

1 to 5 can be used as a build-up to the group activity 6.

1   Move to the tambourine as toy soldiers.

2   With partners, working on the spot. Using the same beat as in 1, one child performs toy soldier movements which his partner has to copy.

3   Repeat 2, changing roles.

4   In pairs make mechanical toys.

5   In pairs make a piece of machinery. Repeat several times, allowing the children to invent different mechanical combinations.

(small groups)

6   Divide the class into groups of five or six each. Working in their own time, each group invents a machine.

The success of this activity is not necessarily the realism of the machine: look also for ingenuity and co-ordination within the group.

If the class does not grasp the idea, the following example of a 'milk bottle machine' will help.

Face two children together, holding both hands: the others are milk bottles on a circular conveyor belt passing through them. The pair holding hands stiffen their arms sideways, and perform a pumping motion, passing through each bottle.

Encourage the children to improve upon this simple machine. When all the groups are active on different machines, the tambourine is not much help. However, if you ask a group to demonstrate their machine, a continuous shake will produce the rattle of moving machinery and should help the performance.

Tied-up Dance   (whole class)

1   The children pretend they are tied hand and foot. Tap out a rhythmical beat and ask them to dance as well as they can.

2   Untie one arm. Dance.

3   Untie the other arm. Dance.

4   Untie one leg. Dance.

5   Untie the other leg. Dance with your whole body.

6   Dance with your fingers; then hands; then arms; then trunk; then knees; then feet—your whole body.

Building up to free dancing in this fashion adds fun and the desire to *want* to dance. Obviously a keen and experienced class will not need this sort of introduction to a dance activity. Alternatively, if the very idea of dancing produces giggles, use the word 'move' not dance. The result will be the same—rhythmical movement to a time-beat.

Work Dances   (whole class)

The teacher can work up to these dances by way of the Tied-up Dance; or build up in stages related to the movement to be used in the dances.

Lumberjack's Dance

Everything is done to a chopping beat on the tambourine.

1   Act being lumberjacks.

2   Saw or chop with a partner.

11

3 Can you make bigger movements and not lose your balance?

4 Can you put in a jump?

5 Take it in turns to copy your partner.

6 Make your movements form a pattern on the floor.

7 Use the movements you like best and make up a lumber-jack's dance.

Policemen's Dance

1 Act being policemen.

2 Act with a partner. (Introduce tambourine beat.)

3 Be traffic policemen. Take it in turns to copy your partner.

4 A traffic policeman usually stands still. Do what he would do, if he could let his feet move in time with his arms.

5 Make up a policeman's dance.

Ask a good pair to demonstrate. Use demonstrations to show the kind of movement that works in dancing. Let the children copy a demonstration if they want to, but do not insist on this. A number may find it helpful to copy; others will want to take their time.

Once the idea of work dances has been established, it will be found that practically any activity can be performed rhythmically, and, if wanted, developed into a dance. The most helpful advice is not to be rigid. If the mood of the class prompts you to develop a mime activity into a dance, then do so. If not, you may care to steer the class into an improvised situation using the activity. Miming coal-miners, for example, could go either way, both right, if the teacher has sensed correctly the mood of the moment.

The following can quickly and simply be turned into dance movement:

sailors	tennis	football
weapon fighting	netball	miners
dustmen	road menders	clowns

Try local occupations, well known to the children.

In addition, children find great fun in trying national dances. Without any special knowledge it is possible to present these in a variety of ways, e.g.

Spanish Cast some as bulls; the rest as toreadors.

Dutch Cast a group as clog makers. The rest buy their clogs and dance away in them.

Scottish Act some events in a highland games.

Russian Divide into boys and girls; each make a large circle. The children clap out the beat, whilst each one takes his turn at doing a few characteristic Russian dance steps in the centre. This is a very good dance for athletic boys.

To a large extent what we wear dictates how we move. Try dancing in:

gumboots   baggy trousers   top hat and tails   space suit a crinoline.

For a change, let the children make up their own dance rhythms. Hand the tambourine round and see what happens. Experiment with a percussion group; leave the group to create its own rhythm and then let the class dance to it. The test here is not finding an occupation for the dance, but simply helping the children to enjoy the sheer pleasure of movement.

Relaxation and Relaxed Movement   (whole class)

Physical tension is a handicap to movement and speech and the teacher should endeavour to overcome this by encouraging activities that need a relaxed body.

Infants, and juniors who have continued with music and movement started as infants, should present no problem. Juniors without this background may well be tense and need encouragement.

The first step is to make sure that the children are happy and enjoying themselves. A discontented child will not relax. Keep a happy atmosphere in the class and all will be well.

Complete relaxation, that is when the body is lying limp on the floor, is easily recognizable. Pick up an arm of this limp body and it will flop back to the floor, a dead weight. Similarly with a leg and the rest of the body. Any tension will be noticed immediately.

Tension may result from a child not being able to 'switch-off' control of a limb: indeed it is not easy to give up command of your body. The object of the following activities is to help the child to achieve this; and to take pleasure in developing easy relaxed movement and complete relaxation without really being aware of it.

Rag Dolls (*pairs*)

One partner acts being a toymaker and makes the other into a rag doll. The toymaker then manipulates his doll—lays it down, folds it up, etc.

Demonstrate how loose and floppy the rag doll has got to be. Take turn about at being the doll.

End the activity with everyone lying on the floor like a rag doll. Suitably relaxing music, or a slow quiet tap on the rim of the tambourine will help.

Wizards (*pairs*)

One child becomes a wizard and controls his partners actions as follows:

After a magic pass, the wizard takes hold of the end of an invisible wire that he has fixed on to the partner's nose and leads him where he will. He can follow this up with other invisible wires, attached where he likes, and so control his partner *without ever touching him*.

Let the wizard go on to invent other controls and mime mixing and administering magic potions. All the wizard's directions should be mimed.

As a development split the class into small groups and mime wizard/mortal situations.

Hypnotists   (pairs)

The partners take turns at being a hypnotist and his subject. This makes use of both speech and mime. The fun of the situation, and the concentration put into his part by the hypnotist, are particularly good for encouraging speech, in addition to relaxation.

Puppets   (pairs)

One partner makes a puppet of the other: he screws together, paints and dresses, and finally operates the puppet.

After everyone has been a puppet, invent a puppet dance. Use appropriate music as an accompaniment or tap out the rhythm on a tambourine.

The Witch Doctor's Surgery   (small groups)

The title will be enough to start the children working and they will need no extra directions. This is another good activity for encouraging relaxed movement and speech: the bizarre treatments prompt active and spontaneous movement and absorption in the character of the witch doctor is an inducement to speech.

Candles   (whole class)

This is useful at the end of a lesson to lead to a period of complete relaxation.

Imagine you are a lighted candle. Slowly melt until you are a pool of wax on the floor.

IN MOVEMENT LOOK FOR AND ENCOURAGE:

Absorption in the activity
Whole floor area used
No unnecessary bumping or touching
Controlled movement and balance
Movement to time-beat and rhythm
Relaxed movement and the loss of tension
Response to directions
Children's own suggestions

Mime

The word 'mime', like the word 'drama', can take on a number of different meanings. For example, we can mime being an aeroplane; we can also mime being people watching that aeroplane crash; and in addition, we can speak in mime, telling a friend about the crash.

Here we see Mime meaning:

1 Acting being something (the aeroplane).
2 Acting an occupation (watching).
3 Replacing the voice by gesture (speech mime).

Normal speech will occur in many mime activities, and, since our aim is to develop language flow, it is desirable to encourage it where possible. (Now and again activities relying solely on speech mime and bodily expression can be used to effect: they are good for stimulating the imagination and physical dexterity.) Don't be tempted to try to 'force' speech, either from a group or a single child. It will appear when they are ready and before long will flow naturally. Conversely, in pure speech mime, turn a blind eye to 'mouthing'; indeed if a child can make himself understood by having his lips read, he is performing an extremely difficult feat well.

The following activities can be linked to many of the movement exercises, allowing the lesson to develop smoothly. The only equipment needed is desks and chairs.

What Am I Doing?   (singly, pairs, or small groups)

The children mime everyday occupations. To start with: What they did before coming to school—getting dressed, brushing hair, washing, cleaning teeth, playing with their favourite toy, etc. Weave the occupations into a simple commentary for them to follow.

When the idea is established, let them mime occupations of their own choice to each other. Make the point that if the mime is guessed first time, it means that it must have been clear and well performed.

To help concentration and clarity, try miming in slow motion, e.g.

dressing. Ask someone to take off a real jersey and let the rest copy in mime.

Which details were left out?

Shops   (pairs or small groups)

The children choose their own kind of shop. For a large group act a supermarket.

If a number of shops are to be in action simultaneously, position them so that the children are encouraged to use all the space available. They will not automatically move from the wall into a larger space.

Build a Town   (whole class)

1   Discuss the jobs, trades, people and occupations in a typical small town. This might possibly be the one the children live in, or near. Using the whole room, plan out the town, casting every member of the class. (This is not so bad as it sounds,

for example some can be cast as groups: factory workers mothers and children, etc.)

Use desks and chairs to suggest different areas. The class then mimes life in the town.

2 As a development, introduce a dramatic occurrence that might affect everyone in the town, for example, a severe snow storm.

3 What else might affect the whole population? Act out the suggestions, encouraging a dramatic atmosphere.

Pairs and Chairs

1 Each pair has a chair. Working turn-about, they mime situations in which the child standing is doing something to, or for, his seated partner, e.g.

> Waiter and diner
> Hairdresser and client
> Dentist and patient
> Salesman and client

2 As a development, adding to the fun and skill, vary the speed of the mimes—normal, fast, slow motion.
To ring the changes, arrange a 'freeze' signal on the tambourine, and then bring them back to life at a new speed.

Film Mimes   (small groups)

This activity springs naturally from Pairs and Chairs, particularly if you have used different speeds. The quick jerky movement of miming at speed suggests the old silent films sometimes seen on TV. Choose a traditional old film situation, e.g.

> A restaurant scene
> A bank raid

21

Furniture removers, who call at the wrong house
Paperhangers
Building a house
Repairing a car

TV Mimes   (small groups)

TV has a strong influence on children and many of their ideas for acting come from it. On occasions items can be copied directly. In mime the simplest way is to let small groups take turns in miming a programme of their choice for the rest of the class to guess.

Try to avoid groups repeating similar items. If a group is acting well, absorbing itself and the audience, let it play on. The TV situation can sometimes provide just the right starting point for a good improvised scene. It won't necessarily happen, but if it does, let it.

Character Mime   (whole class)

1   The idea here is to help the children concentrate on important detail. They should understand that a good character mime is like a good drawing: only the essentials are sketched in. Knowing this, and that the way we move is dictated by the clothes we wear, we can begin to 'sketch' simply and effectively in mime. To help the children understand this, ask them to mime putting on and moving in:

heavy boots   tight shoes   a heavy overcoat
a top hat   a suit of armour   a long cloak
Think of other clothes that alter our movement.

2   We can now start to sketch a particular character. One way to do this with the whole class is as follows:
Show me a large box in front of you.

Take out a large pair of baggy trousers. Hold them up. Put them on. Can you feel them on? They have got stretchy braces—feel them. Put your thumbs in them—stretch them.

Take out a very large pair of clown's boots. Put one of them on, remembering to lace it up. What does it feel like? Put the other one on. How do you stand in your baggy trousers and boots?

Take out a clown's nose. Stick it on. Does it alter your face?

Take out a battered old hat and put it on.

Now you are a clown. Show how he moves about.

Invent a clown's trick with a partner.

(One could add many other details—shirt, tie, socks, etc.— but these tend to confuse. Confine the sketch to essentials.)

You may find it helpful to do the dressing part in slow motion to avoid the mime becoming garbled.

3 The clothes box can be used for numerous characters: e.g. farmer; soldier; dancer; witch; etc.

Sometimes objects ('props') are necessary to the sketch, e.g. window cleaner's bucket; soldier's rifle. Treat these as costume and include them in the dressing up.

4 Work in pairs. One dresses, the other guesses.

Increase to groups guessing each others characters.

All mime scenes do not need to be prefaced with the characters dressing themselves. This activity is to help the children to think about what makes people different from each other.

The Silent Game   (pairs)

The aim is communication without speech and the children can use any other means they like in order to communicate. These will range from simple gestures, to complicated 'acting-out'. No matter what form is chosen, the need for clarity will soon become apparent.

Many subjects are suitable for this kind of exchange, e.g.

1 *Do what I say*. (The partner performs the mimed command.)

2 *Bring me* . . .

3 *I like . . . What do you like?*

4 *Play with my toys.*

5 *Sums*. (The partners take turn about to set each other simple sums on their fingers.)

6 *What am I* . . . smelling? touching? tasting? looking at? listening to?

7 *Shopping.*

8 *Over the garden wall* (two neighbours chatting).

Groups and Leaders

Divide the class into groups of 4, 5 or 6 children in each. Give each child a number (e.g. six children per group, number them 1, 2, 3, 4, 5, 6). When you call out a number, everyone with that number takes command of the group and issues mimed instructions. He can turn the group into what he likes, e.g. a band; a gym class; old people; dancers; puppets; animals.

Continue until everyone has had a turn as leader.

The activity improves if done to music.

People and Places   (whole class)

After naming a place, hold a brief discussion to bring out the possibilities it offers for acting. The following appeal to the imagination:

a forest   a desert island
Iceland   a jungle
a strange planet   the prairie

It is worth noting that dramatic action does not necessarily mean fighting and gun battles. It can also mean the creation of an interesting and compelling atmosphere: an atmosphere of suspense; tension; heat; cold; comedy; or simply the feeling that an interesting story is about to be told.

A number of methods can be used for involving the class in a place:

1   They act what they feel in a certain place.

2   Change from one place to another.

3   Use music and sound effects.

4   Speak a commentary as the children make a journey through the place.

5   Nominate leaders to lead groups on this expedition.

6   Act the inhabitants of the place.

7   Split the class up into small groups to make up stories for acting about the place.

It will help if the children are encouraged to consider the following questions:

Who is there?   Why are they there?

What are they doing?   What are they like?

The answers do not need to be given to the teacher, but they should emerge when the children are discussing amongst themselves the story they are about to act.

The Senses   (small groups)

Our actions and reactions are conditioned by our five senses, and they are therefore important in acting.

Imagine that there are five people called Sharp Eyes; Sharp Fingers; Sharp Ears; Sharp Tongue; Sharp Nose.

1 Act what happened when they went into the forest looking for a witch.

2 Act what happened when they got lost in the mountains.

3 Act what happened when they planned a burglary.

4 Make up your own story about them and act it.

Let the children interpret these literally if they want to, e.g. Sharp Nose, with a long sharp nose.

Vehicles (small groups)

1 Place 4 chairs in the shape of a vintage car. Four children go for a ride, one in front acting as driver. Quite simply, they act the vibrations of the vehicle. They all rise together going over a humpback bridge and incline one way or the other when the car turns, etc. Their success depends on everyone doing the same thing at the same time. To achieve this, the driver is made the leader and the others take their movements from him.

Once the effect has been established and the children understand the technique, the mime can be enlarged to include the sort of detail you would expect on such a journey, e.g. trouble starting the car, a puncture, packing the picnic basket, and so on.

A musical, or rhythmic backing is helpful.

2 The same technique can be used for a variety of vehicles:
a bus   a train compartment and corridor   a lorry
a tank   a boat.

It is important that the children should *see*, and therefore understand, the effect. Let the groups perform to each other. Indicate where the effect of moving succeeds.

3 Act a story about a journey on which something mysterious happens (with or without speech).

26

Friends   (pairs)

1   Two friends take part in a common occupation, for example, camping. The mime starts with the friends in bed in their respective houses. The alarm clock goes. They rise, dress, wash, clean their teeth, have breakfast, pack their gear, leave the house, and meet. They set off for the country—by bike, bus, or train. Once arrived they sort out a camping site, pitch their tent and cook a meal. During their camping they are interrupted by a thunderstorm, and visited by some cows in the night . . . (Many other things can happen. Let them decide.)

    Music goes well with this activity. If you use the piano, they can take their cues from it, e.g. alarm clock, storm, bed. If they perform without music, arrange tambourine signals. Telescope time: it will not worry the children.

2   Vary the character of the pair, keeping the same time pattern, e.g. two workmen (get up, dress, breakfast, meet, start work, lunch break, work, home, bed)

    two nurses
    two soldiers
    two waitresses
    two old men

3   Dispense with the time pattern. Throw more emphasis on to the background and atmosphere:

    two burglars breaking into a house
    two who find themselves in the professor's laboratory
    two mountaineers
    two astronauts on a strange planet

Ready-made Stories   (small groups)

Nursery rhymes and fairy stories provide ready-made plots for mime plays. In the case of rhymes, the rhyme can be spoken whilst the action is taking place. If the rhyme calls for only a small number of characters, let the children act inanimate objects. e.g. Humpty Dumpty's wall; Jack and Jill's well.

Fairy stories can be treated in the same way.

IN MIME LOOK FOR AND ENCOURAGE:

Absorption
Well observed detail
Precise use of gesture
Working away from walls and confidence in the use of space
Co-ordinated group work
The desire to use speech
Children's own suggestions

Improvised Plays

The activities in this section are designed to encourage the children to improvise dialogue in their own plays. It is hoped that the ideas given will appeal to the imagination and spark off spontaneous play-making. Although this is very much the children's own activity, *some* directions do need to be given by the teacher, e.g. the use of space; props; casting. They will vary, of course. The general rule is to keep directions down to the bare minimum.

The class may or may not have used improvised speech in the previous activities. If they have not, it will not automatically occur in the following. Do not be disappointed if the children continue to mime, or speak in whispers. Speech will come, and it will flow, given time and the right encouragement. Sometimes the best encouragement is for the teacher to say nothing at all. (No one can be pressured into natural speech.) They will soon decide that a play is more interesting to do if they 'speak the story'. Television is a help in this respect. It is their most immediate source of reference for plays and acting, and the children will often want to act TV-type situations, in which, fortunately, speech is essential. Similarly there are other situations in which speech is necessary, e.g. a teacher-class scene.

The Performance of Improvised Plays

Most adults' notion of theatre is of an audience watching the performance of a play on a proscenium stage. They see a picture

31

frame, raised and removed from the spectators, complete with a curtain to indicate the beginning and end of things. This method of presentation is quite wrong for the acting of children's improvized plays and should not be used. Indeed the principle that a play must *always* be performed before an audience does not apply to the kind of drama we are concerned with. It *can* be acted out before the rest of the class, but the children should be dissuaded from the belief that this is the inevitable result of making up a play. The main reason for this apparent stricture is that the children are most relaxed and creative when not on display. A group left to itself to make up a play, sheds inhibitions and gains in confidence and language flow.

There are other good reasons for not insisting on always performing before an audience. Extroverts will consciously 'play to' the audience, and consequently not stretch themselves imaginatively. Quieter children may tend to become more self-conscious and nervous as a result of being seen to be at a loss for words.

Of course many children will want to act their plays for the others, and such performances *can* be beneficial to all concerned, providing the teacher is aware of the above. One method of getting the most out of a performance is to reduce the separation between actors and spectators. Aim at informality and avoid the feeling of separation created by a raised stage and proscenium arch.

For example, let us assume that five playmaking groups have all been working on their own plays in the hall. One of the groups wants to show its play to the rest. Rather than clear a special place for the 'stage', simply ask the audience to gather round the area the group is already working in and sit down. If the audience can sit in a rough circular shape around the group, so much the better. (This tends to fuse actors and audience together, cutting out a 'them' and 'us' relationship.) Ideally the feeling emerges that the players and spectators are all part of the same activity. Under these circumstances the actors will often move into, through, and behind the audience, emphasizing the all-in-it-together atmosphere.

32

Performances also help the teacher. From them she can assess progress and the development of individuals. However this is not necessarily the only test, or the best test, in judging some children's progress. Moving amongst the groups, chatting informally, listening to a child's *story* of the play, will reveal a great deal. Enthusiasm for the story will thrust aside shyness and the words will come tumbling out. It will help the child if you can listen on the child's own physical level (stoop, kneel, or sit): you become a confidant, not someone separated by your height. It is not easy to be natural looking up with your head bent back; and the nearer a friendly teacher comes towards you, the more you have to bend back and look up.

It is worth remembering that the benefit from drama may be best seen in other lessons. Look for an improvement in self-confidence and language flow when taking the class for other subjects. *This* is the test.

Working Conditions

Space

A hall, gym, or large empty classroom is best. Whatever the size of the group, always work towards its using the maximum space available. The children will not do this naturally: their usual inclination is to hug the walls, or use nooks created by furniture. If you do not watch this, all the best acting will be done behind the piano. A sure indication of the emergence of self-confidence, is a child's not being afraid of acting in an open space.

If more than one group is working at a time, space them so that each has a fair distribution of floor area to work in. You will notice that in a class of say, 36, it is possible for the groups to work side by side on six different plays quite harmoniously. The harmony can actually be seen in the controlled physical pattern of the whole class co-operating in the use of space.

Furniture and Rostra

The most useful school furniture is stools, chairs, strong desks, gym benches, and if available, rostra. Do not give too much furniture to a group: concern with it will detract from concern for the play. For example, a group given 30 chairs to suggest a fort would happily use them all, taking great care in their arrangement. Its imagination would be directed to making the chairs *look* like a fort, not to inventing a story that takes place in the fort. Obviously some play subjects will need more furniture than others, but the general rule should be to give too little, rather than too much. Make sure that the children know what they can and cannot use, and so avoid having to interrupt a group to prohibit the use of some equipment.

Costume and Props

These too can stand between the child and the invention of an imaginative story. Often costume and props are more of a hindrance than a help. Given the chance, of course, the class will clamour for them. A compromise solution is to allow the children *one* prop, or piece of costume in the *occasional* play.

If a child has to cope with an unusual costume or props, he will tend to concern himself solely with the managing of these and not with the acting of the play. For example, a group of girls acting a tea-party scene would, given the opportunity, provide a dolls' tea service and prop food. The actual managing of small plastic cups and saucers etc. is difficult, and would absorb their effort to the detriment of the improvised dialogue.

If props and costumes are used, check that *a* they are simple, *b* they can be handled easily, and *c* they can be put on quickly.

Size of Groups

This will vary depending on the type of improvised work you choose for the lesson. If the children are going to act a story you have told them, or do an acting project, the group may well be the whole class. Alternatively, an improvised play based on, say, a title, or an object, is best tackled by a small group of no more than six. In this last example, the creative process is much more intense than in the former (there the story, or framework of the story, has been given) and close liaison is needed between the members of the group.

The question of boys and girls working in the same group has to be considered, and the only general answer is that it depends upon the children and the teacher's estimation of the possible success of any particular combination. Forcing boys and girls together against their will is not conducive to work which, by its nature, is dependent upon co-operation. For some plays segregation is beneficial. As an aim, however, it seems reasonable to encourage boys and girls to work together without self-consciousness.

Length of Plays

Plays not being performed before an audience are as elastic as a children's game in the playground: often they just 'happen' and do not end until the actors have tired of the subject. However if performed for the rest of the class the play cannot be allowed to go on and on. Occasionally a group will hit on a story that has dramatic shape and an appropriate dénouement on which to end. As the children gain in experience, one hopes that this will happen more frequently. Until it does, the teacher needs to end the performance at what he judges to be the right moment. A play performed by a small group may last up to 12 minutes, even longer if the dialogue is flowing exceptionally well. The teacher must assess how well the story is developing. The interest level of the audience is another important consideration.

To help the audience (and you), ask one of the group to announce where the play takes place and tell a little about it. This will help everyone to follow the story more easily. Start the play when the audience is quiet and attentive. If the play is obviously not going to end of its own volition, warn the group that they should start to bring it to an end. The direction 'One minute to go', will achieve this with minimum distraction and allow a conclusion to be reached.

When the whole class is acting a story, or an acting project, more time will be needed. Here the activity should reach its natural conclusion without interruption, providing the teacher has made the ending clear.

Speech and Language

The children will speak in their native dialect and it is desirable that they should. Initially it is only through their habitual speech that they will conquer self-consciousness and behave naturally. The artificial speech imposed upon children in the speaking of 'recitations' and acting in scripted plays, is the opposite of what improvised drama sets out to achieve.

The best aid is enjoyment. If the children are enjoying themselves they will be at ease and relaxed, and disposed to let language flow. At this stage, the teacher should be concerned to turn on the tap, not purify the water.

Suggestions for improvised plays

Situations   (small groups)

Two burglars are cycling along on a wet and windy night. They see an old rambling house and decide to break in. They carefully hide their bikes, check their tools and then sneak up to the house and break in. Once in, they sense a curious atmosphere. They explore. As they do, some ghosts emerge from the shadows and watch them. The burglars find a safe but, as they are opening it, the ghosts catch them. The ghosts make the burglars their servants. The first thing the burglars are ordered to do is prepare the ghosts' supper and serve it.

Two girls get lost in the woods. Mist comes down and it gets darker. As they are stumbling along they come to a clearing, in which a witches' school is in session. They watch, fascinated. The chief witch is teaching spell-making. One of the witches is sleepy. After a while, one of the girls sneezes and the witches discover them. The witches have to decide what to do with the girls—one witch wants to turn them into a school dinner. While the witches are arguing, the girls manage to look in a spell book and what they read helps them to escape.

A group of men are setting off on a pot-holing expedition. They check their gear and supplies on the surface, then lead off. They progress through a large cave, then come to an underground river. They inflate a dinghy and paddle along. Next they come to a maze of small passages. One of the group gets lost. There is a rock fall, one man is injured. The remainder of the group form themselves into a rescue party to find the lost man and bring him and the injured man to the surface. Eventually they are successful.

A group of girls (or boys) is going camping. They call at the house of a friend who is going with them. But she is still in bed asleep . . . dreaming of the camping expedition she is going on with her friends. We see the topsy-turvy expedition she dreams.

A member of a resistance group has informed to the enemy and must be killed. The assassin is chosen by the drawing of lots. The play takes place in a cellar, the door of which is locked and covered with a heavy curtain. There is a secret knock, known only to the group. The play starts with the leader and the crippled man who guards the door, alone in the cellar.

One night a flying saucer lands in a field. In a nearby house a group of teenagers are having a party. They go out to explore when they hear the strange noise of the saucer. Eventually the saucer-people meet the teenagers, who discover that they are friendly. The only difference is that the saucer-people do not speak our language and walk sideways. The teenagers try to explain our way of life to the saucer-people and invite them to their party, at which they have been dancing and playing games.

A family party sets out in a car for a picnic on the shore of Loch Ness. The children go fishing while the grown-ups get the picnic ready. The children catch the Loch Ness monster. They rush back to tell the grown-ups who will not believe them and scold them for being naughty. The children go back to the monster, who turns out to be friendly. They persuade him to come with them to meet the grown-ups.

A prince once found a magic bottle. When he tapped it, a genie appeared and granted all his wishes. However the prince was very greedy and never satisfied. In the end, he was destroyed by his greediness.

The scene is Switzerland. A mother and father take their twins to market to buy them a sledge for their birthday. Returning home the family is greeted by the dog. When the twins are tucked into bed, the dog tries to get in as well. He is put out and the parents retire. When the house is asleep the twins get up and plan to try out their new sledge. They creep out of the house and take the sledge up the mountain. They stumble over a cliff of snow and land on a ledge. The dog wakes and goes to the twins' bedroom and discovers they are not there. He finally manages to show the parents what is wrong. Mother gets the Alpine police and they, father and dog, track down the twins and rescue them. As his reward the dog is allowed to sleep on the twins' bed.

A team of quarrymen are working on a hillside. With care and efficiency they lay a charge of dynamite and prepare to detonate it. After the explosion, they find that an unknown cave has been revealed. Taking lamps with them, they start to explore the cave, which goes deeper and deeper. Ultimately their trek leads them into pre-history and the time of the Stone-Age cave dwellers . . .

A team of explorers has disappeared. Another expedition plans to discover what happened to them. They set out on their journey (polar, tropical, or mountain) and eventually achieve radio contact with the lost party. The expedition is warned of the dangers in store if they attempt a rescue operation. They disregard the warning and set about rescuing their friends.

Plays from Class Projects   (small groups)

Let the group choose one of the projects the class has worked on. Appoint a leader. The group is given five minutes to think of as many words as it can connected with the subject of the project. The leader lists these down. When the time is up, the group is asked to choose one or two words from the list as the starting off point for a story. (The story is *not* written down.)

Point out that the whole story may develop from the beginning word(s) without further reference to the list. If, however, the story 'dries up', refer back to the list, where there is certain to be a word to set the story in motion again.

Act the story.

In fact the children do not often dry up. The compiling of the list stirs the memory and the imagination: by the time they start on the story they are already full of ideas.

History, geography, science, and local study projects, all lend themselves to this treatment.

Titles   (small groups)

Make up and act stories with these titles:
    The Suspect
    Smugglers' Gold
    Oh!—What a Surprise!
    The Sleepy Teacher
    The Curse of the Mummy's Tomb
    Journey into the Unknown
    The *Unlucky* Rabbit's Foot
    The Well-planned Robbery that Went Wrong
    Filming Wild Life in Africa (something goes wrong)

In choosing a title try to make it suggest the possibility of physical action. *Doing* leads to absorption, which leads to speech.

Object Plays   (small groups)

Give the group an object and ask the children to make up a story for acting about the object. Collect slightly bizarre objects, which
40

will offer the possibility of fantasy. Such objects are numerous but might include:

an ornate fan	a Tyrolean pipe
an evening bag	a cornucopia
a man's wallet	a pince-nez
a monocle	a riding crop
a snuff box	a walking stick
ballet shoes	a wig
strings of beads	castanets

Pantomimes and Fairy Stories   (small groups)

Choose a pantomime or fairy story for acting, e.g.

Cinderella	Robinson Crusoe
Alladin	The Sleeping Beauty
Hansel and Grethel	Rumpelstiltskin
Red Riding Hood	Snow White

Three Words   (small groups)

Make up a story for acting about any of these groups of three:

highlands	Eskimos	undergrowth	granny
water	food	heat	surprise
winter	blizzard	fear	children
hospital	cake	scouts	foreign
fire engine	tears	mystery	confusion
telephone	presents	tent	solution

One Word   (small groups)

Act a story about each word:
>   suspicion   lucky   magic   hunger   revenge   marooned
>   sky   Saturday   plan   Christmas

Instant Scenes   (small groups)

The following can be acted without preparation before the rest of the class.

A train compartment. Each be a different person on a train journey. Use chairs to make the compartment and mime the sliding doors and narrow corridor. One of the travellers is an awkward person and the others find him a nuisance.

A country bus. Make the bus with chairs and act the people travelling on it. It is an old, bumpy bus, and after a while it breaks down.

An air terminal. People from different countries are arriving and departing. The airport official is not very efficient, but he does his best to help the travellers.

A group of pets meet together and discuss how they look after their owners.

A pet show. Some owners are getting their pets ready for

the judging. (Each is sure that his is best.) The judge announces that he has never seen such a miserable bunch of animals in his life.

A car park. Four cars are parked close together in a car park: a vintage car, a land rover, a sports car, and a family saloon. They talk about each other and how their owners treat them.

Over the garden wall. Two neighbours are gossiping about the shortcomings of a third. The third neighbour appears.

There are two twins: one is invisible. They see a policeman. The invisible twin plays tricks on him and tells his brother to try—it's easy . . .

A hypnotist hypnotizes his patient and tells him what to do and talk about.

A man is proudly washing his new car. His know-all neighbour arrives and proceeds to show him what is wrong with the car, and then tries to show him how to take it to pieces and put it right.

A teacher is taking a class. One of the older boys has brought a forbidden transistor radio to school. The class has to keep the radio hidden from the teacher.

A ventriloquist and his doll.

Stories for acting by the whole class

The following are four examples of stories that can be acted by a whole class or large group. It is desirable that the stories for this activity should provide clearly understood locations and physical action: the children should be 'doing', and know where the doing is supposed to be taking place.

Having selected a suitable story, use this method of presentation:

1   Read the story to the class.

2   Check that the children have followed the main outline of the story. Don't let this process take too long.

3   Cast the story. (Having made sure beforehand that there is a need for groups.)

4   Indicate where the locations will be, and say what furniture can be used.

5   As soon as the children are in their opening locations, start the play.

6   Leave them to get through as well as they can.

7   After the first time through, ask the children if they have any improvements to suggest and remind them of any part of the story that was left out.

8   Act the story again.

How the sea became salty

Many years ago there was a king of Denmark called King Frodi and he had been given a huge pair of millstones. Now these millstones were enchanted and they would grind out anything the owner desired. Unfortunately for the King, however, not even his strongest men could turn them. After nearly worrying himself to death, King Frodi at last managed to buy two giantesses as slaves. The moment he got them back to his castle he set them to work, ordering them to grind out peace, prosperity, and gold.

The giantesses worked well. But the richer the King grew, the greedier he became. The giantesses begged for a little rest, but the King refused with brutal threats. Day and night they were forced to keep the great mill going.

At last, it was more than the giantesses could endure. One night, instead of bidding the millstones grind out wealth and peace, they sang a song of ruin and war. And so while the Danes were asleep, a host of Vikings came up from the shore, surrounded the castle and killed the King and his warriors. Then Mysinger, the Viking Chief, took the giantesses and the millstones on board his ship and set sail for home.

Mysinger was also selfish and he wanted to be made rich at once, so he soon set the giantesses to work. They were ordered to grind salt, which in those days was rare and precious. When there was a good pile, the giantesses asked if they might rest, but the Viking Chief refused, and still with aching arms they had to push the great millstones round and round.

Before long such mountains of salt had been produced that the ship looked like a floating iceberg. Then—without warning—there was a cracking of timbers, a terrible lurch, and the overladen vessel sank with all on board.

The sea has been salty ever since. As for the poor giantesses, they were so tired that they were thankful to sleep, even on the bed of the ocean.

Cast	King Frodi	Two Giantesses
	Two Millstones	Chief Mystinger
	Frodi's strongest men	Viking Warriors

Locations	Area for the castle
	Where the giantesses are bought
	Area for Viking ship

(Note: The Vikings mime silently in their ship until after the giantesses grind out their war song.)

Why the Indians live in peace

A wise chieftain once lived in an Indian village. Through the years he had come to realize that the Indians were not born to fight and die: what they really wanted was to work in peace. One day the chieftain called a meeting of the whole tribe and told his people that the first Indian who had lifted his tomahawk against his brother was a bad Indian.

The others saw that he was right and they decided not to paint their faces and set out on the war path. 'But who will carry the message of peace to the neighbouring tribe?' they asked.

The chieftain replied that this would be done by Silent Moccasin and Swift Stag. So, early next morning, the two braves set out. Soon they came to a large wood. Fallen trees, thorny bushes and swamps barred their way. Eventually they managed to get through and soon after reached the neighbouring village. Before entering the village, they carefully buried their weapons.

Seeing that the braves had no weapons and were not wearing paint, the villagers took them to their chief. They then delivered their peace message.

After consulting with his warriors, the chief spoke: 'I accept your proposal. Let us meet in four days time in the big meadow halfway between our two camps. There we shall dig a pit, and in it we shall throw all our war weapons. Then we shall shake hands and live like brothers for all time.'

Silent Moccasin and Swift Stag returned home through the big wood and told their own chief the good news.

In four days time the two tribes met at the big meadow. They dug a pit and faced each other across it. The chieftains were the first to step forward. Both threw their tomahawks into the pit and shook hands. The others followed their example and when the last had thrown away their weapons, they lit fires and danced in celebration.

Cast	First Chief	Second Chief
	Silent Moccasin	Warriors
	Swift Stag	Squaws
	Warriors	
	Squaws	

Locations	First Village (one half of hall)
	Second Village (the other half of hall)
	The Wood

(The Wood is made by *everyone*, except the two braves, in the centre of the hall. When the braves have passed through, the others revert to being Indians. This is repeated on the return journey.)

The first men in England

There was once a tribe of primitive people who lived beside a broad river. Across the river, there was a jungle full of game: but on its own side of the river, the tribe had great difficulty in finding any food at all. When the river was not too fierce, some of the men would swim across and hunt food, and then they would return with what they could manage to haul across.

As the tribe grew larger, this way of providing food was not sufficient. The leader of the tribe held a meeting and it was decided that somehow or other, the whole tribe should move to the other side of the river and live there. They could not all swim and there was another problem: how were they going to take their fire? Since they did not know how to make fire, it was important that they preserved the fire they had. It was decided to construct a huge raft of logs, in the centre of which they would make a clay container for the fire.

The making of the raft took a long time. Cutting down trees with crude flint axes was a never ending job and they had to devise another way of providing the timber. The leader had the idea of hollowing out small holes in the base of the trees and keeping fires burning in them. This they did and one night, while they were sleeping, a strong wind blew the weakened trees down. When the tribe saw what had happened, they held a celebration, and then set to work completing the raft.

Eventually they set sail, complete with their fire and landed safely on the other side of the river where they built a village of branches and skins. Since that day, thousands of years ago, the river has broadened itself and is now known as the English Channel. The tribe's new country became known as England.

Cast	Wild Animals	Men
	Swimming Hunters	Women
	The Leader	Children

Locations	The tribe's village by the river
	The river
	The jungle on the other side

Buccaneers

A buccaneer ship sights a small Spanish town on the coast of South America. The buccaneers plan to raid the town. They are successful and when installed in the town they demand wine and festivities. These are provided by the mayor and the townspeople, apparently anxious to please their conquerors. While the dancing is in full swing, it becomes clear that the mayor has a plan—to make sure that the buccaneers have far too much to drink.

The mayor's plan succeeds. Only with the greatest difficulty do the buccaneers manage to stagger back to their ship. Once on board, they fall sound asleep.

The mayor gathers together a raggle taggle army of townspeople and leads a reprisal against the buccaneer ship. The buccaneers offer no resistance and the mayor's band take them as prisoners back to the town.

There are more festivities, but this time it is the buccaneers who have to serve the townspeople. Eventually the mayor strikes a bargain with the buccaneer captain. In return for the forfeit of his ship, the buccaneers will be given their freedom. The buccaneers decide to stay in the town and live peacefully.

Cast	Captain	Mayor
	Buccaneers	Townspeople

Locations	The ship
	The sea
	The town

Act the story in scenes:

1 *The ship* The buccaneers sight the town and plan the raid.

2 *The town, evening* A wedding celebration is just ending. Sentries are posted. The town sleeps.

3 *The sea and town* The buccaneers attack and the town surrenders. Wine, song and dance.

4 *The sea and ship* The buccaneers return.

5 *Town, sea and ship* The reprisal.

6 *Town, festivities* The bargain is made.

Acting Projects for the whole class

Choose a theme that can be expressed in speech and action by small groups working in co-operation with each other. Allow rehearsal time for the individual groups before co-ordinating.

The following are three examples of suitable subjects and how they are put into practice.

Rescue at Sea

Hold a discussion about communications at sea. Let the class become aware of the communications network.

Make up a network and give each group its part to play, e.g.

Trawler

Lifeboat

Air/Sea Rescue
Helicopter

Meteorological Office

Shore Radio

The Shore Radio is in radio and telephone contact with the rest and acts as central control.

Each group makes up its unit with the furniture allowed.

The activity starts with normal daily routine.

1 Meteorological office compiling and issuing weather forecasts.
   Air/Sea rescue crew servicing their helicopter.
   Trawler fishing and reporting position.
   Lifeboat crew at their daily work.
   Shore Radio making routine position and weather calls.

2   The weather gets worse.
    Lifeboat and helicopter are placed on Standby.

3   Gale force winds reported in trawler's area.

4   The trawler sends out MAY DAY distress signal.

5   Emergency Stations. Lifeboat and helicopter are sent out.

6   Shore Radio acts as liaison and controls the rescue operation.

7   The lifeboat rescues the crew. One man falls into the sea, but is winched to safety by the helicopter.

8   The Met. office group change into a TV crew and film and interview the rescued men when they are brought ashore.

Television Magazine Programme

The items are introduced by a centrally situated Link-man. The teacher plays the part of the Floor Manager, cueing-in and winding up items by mimed signals.

Examples of group items

1   A dockers' leader addressing a strike meeting.

2   Four teenagers questioning a pop singer.

3   A film star arriving at London Airport, being met by fans and interviewed.

4   Four students being interviewed about their journey across Europe in an old taxi.

5   Prize fight with commentary.

6   The weather forecast.

7   What's on tomorrow.

Let the groups discuss and plan their item. Before they go on the air, the Link-man visits each group and jots down information about them for his introductions.

51

When on the air, each item is taken in turn. Establish the atmosphere of a television studio—everyone involved, but quiet, waiting for their starting cue from the Floor Manager.

Agricultural Show

Each group represents a stand at the show, e.g.

      Tractor stand
      Auction ring
      Women's Institute crafts
      Refreshment stand
      Farm machinery
      Country dancing
      Show jumping
      Garden plants
      Pets corner
      Dairy produce

A foreign visitor is taken round the show. He does not understand English very well and each group explains its stand to him.

IN IMPROVISED PLAYS LOOK FOR AND ENCOURAGE:

Absorption
Language flow
Creative group work
Imaginative characters and situations
The understanding of what makes a good story
Children's own suggestions

'It is the making of drama that has the most to contribute to the development of children, and its importance is such that it should have a regular place at all stages. By being provided with opportunities for self-expression, the child is given an outlet for his feelings and helped to gain some control over his emotions. By identifying himself with other people, real or imagined, by acting out situations within his experience or his imaginative range, by expressing in movement and speech the feelings of himself and of others, he is enlarging his experience, and learning in ways that are natural to him.'

From the report PRIMARY EDUCATION IN SCOTLAND